Festive Chocolate

Recipes by
Peter G. Rose

Illustrations by
Sandra Baenen

PETER PAUPER PRESS, INC.
WHITE PLAINS • NEW YORK

Table of Contents

Introduction

Although the rich taste of chocolate has been loved for centuries, it has only recently become a national passion. In 1984 the average American ate over 10 pounds of chocolate, possibly for its nourishment but mostly for its smooth, silky, sensuous quality.

Festive Chocolate combines treasured existing recipes with others created especially for this book, menus for chocolate parties, chocolate history and facts, and tips on preparation of chocolate. Mosaic Cookies, Deep Fried Chocolate Ice Cream and Norman's Dream are just some examples of sinfully delicious ways of using chocolate. These and other simple, tested recipes will bring impressive results.

Special thanks to Country Epicure's International Pastry Arts Center in Bedford Hills, New York for permission to use Chef Albert Kumin's chocolate manual for technical information and to my wonderful friend, Andrea Candee, who devised most of the drink recipes. Final thanks to my daughter, Peter Pamela, who helped with the testing; it's great to share something you love with someone you love.

P.G.R.

A LITTLE BIT OF HISTORY

The Spaniards turned up their noses at those ugly brown beans Christopher Columbus sent home from his fourth trip to the New World. However, after Hernán Cortés several decades later brought back the knowledge of how to use the scorned beans, chocolate rapidly became a favored drink of Spanish royalty.

By the end of the 17th Century there were chocolate houses in France, Holland and England, and chocolate was the ''in'' drink of the well-to-do.

In 1765 James Baker established the first chocolate factory in North America, to the delight of Thomas Jefferson, who hoped that ''the superiority of chocolate both for health and nourishment will soon give it the same preference over tea and coffee in America which it has in Spain.''

Through the centuries chocolate has been hailed for its special qualities—as an aphrodisiac (the Aztecs), as a cure for fevers or to prolong life, and as a quick energy food (the US Army).

Once chocolate was established as a drink, discoveries were made that turned it into a ''food.'' The Dutch found a way to make cocoa powder and the Swiss invented milk chocolate. Most subsequent improvements had to do with mechanization, and the Hershey Company now claims that its chocolate bars are "untouched by human hands."

THE MANUFACTURE OF CHOCOLATE

Cacao trees grow in semi-tropical climates and yield about 7-8 pounds of cocoa seeds per year. The fruit, with its 50 beans per pod, has to be an orange color and completely ripe before it is harvested.

The cocoa beans are placed in fermenting boxes and covered by banana leaves. Fermentation takes 2-3 days depending on temperature, and it prevents the beans from becoming bitter, gives them a reddish color, and mellows their flavor. After this process, the beans are washed, dried, packed and shipped.

When the beans arrive at the factory they are first cleaned and selected, then roasted in hermetically-sealed ovens. After roasting, the shells are cracked open, the husks are removed and the beans are crushed and ground. This produces "chocolate liquor," the base ingredient for all chocolate and cocoa.

Cocoa butter is extracted from the chocolate liquor under high pressure, leaving a residue of chocolate press cake which is ground to make cocoa powder. Additional (and varying) amounts of cocoa butter added to the chocolate liquor, together with sugar and sometimes flavorings, produce the candy we all know and love. The lengthy process of conching or continuous kneading creates the much-desired smooth, melt-in-the-mouth quality that makes chocolate so special.

The only secret in the manufacture of different chocolates lies in the combination of beans that are used. The Swiss combine beans from several countries; the Dutch stick to Asian beans; the Spanish prefer Brazilian beans; and the French use beans from Africa.

TYPES OF CHOCOLATE

Chocolate Liquor: made from raw chocolate after the grinding and pressing procedures.

Bitter Chocolate (baking chocolate): hardened chocolate liquor.

Bittersweet Chocolate: 50% chocolate liquor and a minimum of sugar.

Semi-Sweet Chocolate: usually has 24-33% sugar added (the more sugar, the less costly the product).

Milk Chocolate: consists of chocolate liquor,

cocoa butter, sugar, milk solids and flavoring. The lighter the chocolate, the higher the percentage of milk solids that has been substituted for cocoa solids, and the less costly the product.

White Chocolate: consists of cocoa butter, sugar, milk solids and vanilla. Some purists say that this is not truly chocolate because it contains no chocolate liquor.

Emulsified Chocolate: Lecithin, an emulsifier, is added, the amount depending upon the manufacturer.

Cocoa Butter: the only fat which when properly stored does not become rancid. It absorbs odors easily.

Cocoa Powder: usually contains 9 1/2-15% cocoa butter; the percentage affects quality and price. Dutch process cocoa has an alkali added, which yields a deep reddish-brown product.

Couverture: European coating chocolate with a high percentage of cocoa butter.

HOW TO WORK WITH CHOCOLATE

In baking, chocolate can be replaced by cocoa, using the following rule of thumb: 3 level TBsps. cocoa + 1 level TBsp. shortening = 1 square of baking chocolate.

In candy-making, remember that chocolate is highly temperamental, and easily influenced by any change in temperature or humidity. The ideal working environment is about 65 degrees F. with 50% or less humidity.

To melt chocolate, use a double boiler but do not let the water in the bottom come to a boil. Any water drops or steam that gets into the chocolate will make it grainy. *Chocolate should be melted slowly, at a temperature for white chocolate no higher than 115 degrees and for dark chocolate no higher than 120 degrees*. Chop chocolate into small pieces, place ⅓ in the top of the double boiler, stir and let melt. Gradually add more chopped chocolate, melt, stir, and continue to add more until all is melted.

As an alternative, you can melt chocolate on a warming tray set on high (as do some professional chocolatiers).

Tempering, a method which requires the raising and lowering of the temperature of melted chocolate, ensures that it sets rapidly and has the warm gloss which looks so appetizing in professionally coated bonbons and other candies. Discussions of how to temper chocolate can be found in books on chocolate candy-making. None of the recipes in this book require tempering.

Finally, you can place chocolate in a small glass or ceramic dish in the microwave for 1½ minutes on high. Then remove and stir to finish melting.

Although these explanations may be a bit daunting, rest assured the recipes that follow are easy to do and well worth the effort. Even if things go wrong, there will never be any waste, because as Sandra Boynton states in *Chocolate, the Consuming Passion* (Workman Publishing, New York, 1982): "unsuccessful fudge makes an excellent ice cream topping; unsuccessful brownies make an unusual and delicious pudding; an unsuccessful chocolate souffle makes an attractive beret."

NOTE: In testing, unsalted butter and Grade A large eggs were used. All baking requires a preheated oven.

Candies

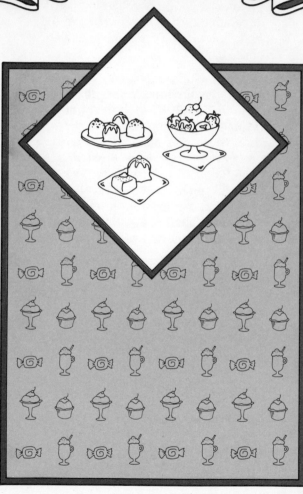

A recipe by professional truffletier Adrienne Welch will give you professional results. Since these truffles are simply rolled in cocoa, the preparation time is very short, approx. 40 minutes. Use the plastic containers from pasta, especially Manicotti, for neatly storing these delicate candies.

CLASSIC TRUFFLES

Ganache (Filling):

½ cup heavy cream
1 vanilla bean, cut in half
A few grains of salt
8 oz. bittersweet chocolate, in 1-inch pieces
1 oz. milk chocolate, in 1-inch pieces
2 egg yolks
1½ TBsps. dark rum or liqueur of your
   choice

Coating:

1½ cups unsweetened cocoa

Combine the heavy cream, vanilla bean, and salt in a small saucepan over medium heat. Bring to a gentle boil. Remove from the heat and allow to cool 5 minutes. While the cream is heating, melt the chocolate (see p.10). Set aside.

Strain the hot cream through a fine sieve into a small mixing bowl. Whisk in the egg yolks and melted chocolate. Add the dark rum or liqueur and blend until smooth. Place the bowl of ganache (filling) in ice water, making sure that the water cannot slosh into the mixture. Stir constantly with a rubber spatula until the ganache is very thick and completely cool (approximately 5 minutes).

Immediately whip the ganache in an electric mixer, using a paddle attachment if you have one, until it lightens in color and forms soft peaks, about 15 to 30 seconds. Do not overbeat or the mixture will harden too quickly and the texture of the truffle will be grainy. Line a baking sheet with foil. Fit a pastry bag with a #8 round tube.

To shape the truffles, spoon half the ganache into the pastry bag. Pipe 6-inch long cylinders onto the baking sheet. Refill the pastry bag and continue to pipe. Refrigerate for 10 minutes to harden the truffles.

Slice the cylinders into 1½-inch pieces. Lightly dust the truffles with 1½ table-spoons unsweetened cocoa. With your fingertips, form each piece into an irregularly shaped 1-inch ball. Roll the truffles in cocoa and store.

A flavorful, easy-to-make candy which tastes like a sweet-shop confection.

CHOCOLATE FRUIT DELIGHT

⅓ cup golden raisins
⅓ cup dark raisins
⅓ cup currants
½ cup water
⅓ cup dark rum
10 oz. semi-sweet chocolate chips
4 TBsps. heavy cream
⅓ cup sliced toasted almonds
10-12 crisp ginger cookies, crushed to
  crumbs

Combine raisins, currants and water. Bring to a boil and simmer for about ten minutes. Drain. Place the plumped fruit in the ⅓ cup of rum. Soak for half hour. Place 2 TBsps. of this marinating liquid in a heavy saucepan together with the chocolate and the cream. Gently melt the chocolate over low heat (see p. 10). When the chocolate is melted, remove from heat, and stir in the almonds and drained fruit. Combine thoroughly. Cool. Shape into 1-inch balls and coat with cookie crumbs.

If you have always wondered what to do with the candied ginger and syrup in its pretty Chinese jar, here is the solution. Combined with walnuts and gingersnap crumbs it makes a lustily-flavored little tidbit, so good you cannot stop eating it.

CHINESE TORTURE

8 pieces candied ginger, finely diced (5 TBsps. after dicing).
3 oz. walnuts, chopped (about 8 TBsps. after chopping)
3 TBsps. ginger syrup
¾ cup ginger snaps, crushed
10 oz. semi-sweet chocolate, melted and cooled slightly (see p. 10)
2 TBsps. cocoa
1 TBsp. superfine sugar

Combine candied ginger, walnuts, syrup, crumbs, and melted chocolate. Form 1-

inch balls. Mix cocoa and sugar. Coat
each ball completely with this mixture.
Wrap and store in refrigerator.

*The combination of the ice-cold, hard choc-
olate coating with the sweet, fragrant fruit
is an ambrosial treat indeed. It is so simple
to do that this will soon become the only
way you serve strawberries.*

CHOCOLATE-COATED STRAWBERRIES

5 oz. bar milk (sweet) chocolate
1 pint of strawberries
7" wooden skewers

Carefully wash the strawberries. (They
usually are quite gritty and might also
have been sprayed with pesticides.)
Leave on the green tops. Pat dry thoroughly with paper towels. Melt the
chocolate in a small dish on a warming
tray (see p.). Spear each fruit on a
skewer, but do not push it all the way
through. Dip each strawberry in the
melted chocolate. Use a small rubber
spatula to spread an even, neat-looking
coating on about three-quarters of the
fruit. Push the skewers into an orange,

grapefruit, or green cabbage (depending on how many you are making). Refrigerate at least an hour until they are ice-cold and the coating is hard. Serve straight from the refrigerator.

A truffle recipe by chef Jane Wong was adapted to make two different batches of truffles. One will give you the Frangelico filling for the Majestic Pears on page 48, plus enough left over ganache (filling) to make about 15 hazelnut-flavored morsels. The second batch gets its intense flavor from Cointreau and grated orange zest and will create 24 truffles.

MELT-IN-YOUR-MOUTH TRUFFLES

1 cup minus 1 TBsp. heavy cream
4 TBsps. butter
1 14-oz. package chocolate chips
4 TBsps. finely chopped walnuts
1 tsp. grated orange zest (use orange part of skin only)
¾ oz. Frangelico (use standard 1-oz. shot glass to measure)
¾ oz. Cointreau (use standard 1-oz. shot glass to measure)
½ cup cocoa

In a double boiler, bring the cream and butter to a boil. Add the chocolate and stir until chocolate has dissolved. This makes 2⅓ cups of ganache (as this truffle mixture is called). Divide into two batches, one of 1⅓ cups, the other of 1 cup. Cool slightly. Add the walnuts to the larger batch. Add the orange zest to the smaller batch. Pour each batch into an 8-inch square pan. Cool. When completely cool, turn larger batch into a bowl. Slowly add the Frangelico while beating the mixture with an electric handmixer. Do not overbeat. Repeat process with second batch, using Cointreau. Reserve about 1½ tablespoons of the Frangelico-flavored ganache for each pear in the Majestic Pear recipe (p. 48). Freeze remaining Frangelico ganache and all of Cointreau ganache. To shape truffles: Remove ganache from freezer. Shape semi-thawed ganache into 1-inch balls, using a melon-ball cutter. Chill. Working with a few at a time, place each truffle into a dish with the cocoa and roll to coat. Keep truffles refrigerated.

Cookies

A substantial cookie which, when filled with a creamy chocolate mint wafer, makes a perfect addition to the lunchbox. As a single cookie, topped with a pecan, it is a lady-like teatime treat.

BUTTER MINT SANDWICHES

½ cup butter
1 cup sugar
1 egg
2 squares unsweetened chocolate, melted
  (see p. 10) and cooled
1 tsp. vanilla
⅓ cup half and half, or heavy cream
2 cups sifted flour
1 tsp. baking powder
½ tsp. salt
Mint-flavored chocolate wafers (such as
  After Eight)
Pecan halves

Cream butter; add sugar gradually; continue creaming until light. Add egg; mix well. Add chocolate and vanilla. Stir in sifted dry ingredients. Shape the dough into a long roll 1½ inches in diameter. Wrap in wax paper and refrigerate one

hour. Remove from refrigerator, unwrap
and cut into slices ⅛-inch thick. For
best results do not make them thicker.
Top some with pecan halves, if desired.
Leave some plain. Bake on ungreased
baking sheets at 375 degrees for 8 minutes. Put a chocolate wafer on some of
the plain cookies as soon as they come
from the oven, then top with another
plain cookie. Cool. Store in airtight container. Makes 36 cookies.

*A crunchy, satisfying small morsel. Not too
much, not too little, it is just right to still
that momentary chocolate craving.*

CHOCOLATE ALMOND CRUNCHIES

½ cup butter, softened
1 TBsp. brown sugar
2 TBsps. white sugar
1 tsp. vanilla
½ cup toasted almonds, chopped
½ cup miniature chocolate chips
1 cup sifted flour

Combine all ingredients and mix thoroughly. Shape into 1-inch balls. Bake at

350 degrees for 15 minutes. Check after 10 minutes (the bottoms tend to burn). Remove from oven and roll into confectioners' sugar while still warm. Makes 36 cookies.

Harriet B. Risley

A beautiful cookie that looks like a lace doily with a delicate chocolate swirl in the middle. These cookies deserve a silver platter.

CHOCOLATE SWIRL LACE COOKIES

8 TBsps. butter, softened
⅔ cup sugar
1 cup flour
½ tsp. vanilla
1 TBsp. cocoa

Cream the butter with the sugar and add the flour. Stir to combine thoroughly. Divide the dough in half. To one half add the vanilla, to the other the cocoa. Roll out each ball of dough into a rectangle of the same size. Place the chocolate dough on top and roll lengthwise— jelly-roll fashion. Refrigerate for 30 minutes. Cut the dough into ¼-inch thick slices. Place the slices 2 inches apart on an ungreased baking sheet. Bake at 350 degrees for 12 minutes. Remove promptly. Makes 36 cookies.

The recipe that follows is based on the principle: "If one is good, two is better." The cookies are packed with chocolate as well as butterscotch chips.

DOUBLE CHIP COOKIES

½ cup butter, softened
1 cup sugar
2 eggs
1 tsp. vanilla
2¼ cups flour
2 tsps. baking powder
¼ tsp. salt
½ cup chocolate mini chips
½ cup butterscotch chips, cut in half

Cream together the butter and sugar. Add the eggs and vanilla and combine thoroughly. Sift together the dry ingredients and add them to the butter mixture. Stir in the chips. Shape the dough into 1-inch balls and place them on a greased baking sheet. Flatten the balls with a floured glass. Bake at 375 degrees for about 12 minutes. They will remain light on top. Remove and cool. Store in an airtight container. Makes 36 cookies.

When you are a favorite aunt with many nieces and nephews you have to know how to make a special treat. "Auntie Bea" is known for her Monster Cookies. She found the recipe decades ago in a farm magazine. The kids love these crispy, flavorful cookies which are a meal in themselves.

MONSTER COOKIES

6 eggs
1 lb. light brown sugar
2 cups white granulated sugar
1 tsp. vanilla
4 tsps. baking soda
1 tsp. corn syrup
1 cup butter, softened
2 cups peanut butter
9 cups oatmeal
½ lb. chocolate chips
½ lb. M&M's
½ lb. M&M peanut candies

Mix in a very large bowl or dishpan in order listed. If you use only half of this

recipe you can mix it in an electric mixer up to the point that the chocolate and
candies are added. Drop a large spoonful
on a greased baking sheet and flatten
with the bottom of the spoon. Place no
more than 6 on a baking sheet (they
run). Bake at 350 degrees for about 10-
12 minutes. Do not overbake. Cool on
baking sheet until hardened. Makes 36
cookies 5-6 inches in diameter.

Vera Johnson

A buttery sand-tart-type cookie with an intri-
cate design. For best results make the
dough a day ahead of baking.

MOSAIC COOKIES

1½ cups butter, softened
1 cup of confectioners' sugar, tapped down
1 egg
1 tsp. vanilla extract
3 cups cake flour, tapped down
1 TBsp. cocoa

Cream the butter and the sugar, add the
egg and vanilla extract. Combine thoroughly. Add the flour and combine to a
soft pliable dough. Divide into three
balls of dough. To one, add the cocoa;

knead into the dough completely. Wrap all three dough balls separately and refrigerate for 12 hours. Remove one white and the chocolate ball and pat or roll each into a small rectangle of 6½" x 3" x ½" thick. Place one on top of the other and cut into ½-inch thick strips. Place two strips beside each other in such a way that chocolate and white dough alternate in checkerboard style. Remove the last dough ball from refrigerator and cut off a small piece. Roll it ⅛-inch thick, big enough to wrap around two strips of dough completely. Proceed in the same manner with the other strips of dough. Wrap each in wax paper and refrigerate for ½ hour. Remove and press down to ensure that outer thin dough wrapping adheres on all four sides of each double strip of dough. Trim ends and cut into ¼-inch slices. Place on ungreased baking sheets. Bake at 350 degrees for 8-10 minutes until delicately browned at the edges. Remove and cool.

Cakes

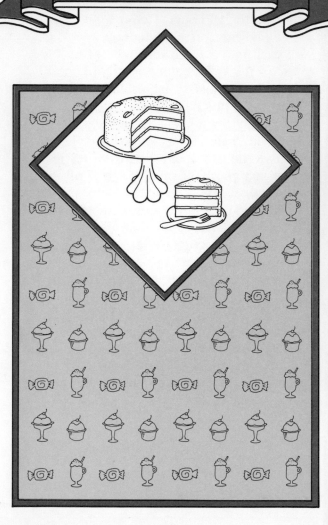

A dense cake with a pronounced cherry flavor

CHERRY CHOCOLATE UPSIDE DOWN CAKE

8 TBsps. butter, divided
⅓ cup + ½ cup white sugar
1 egg
¼ cup milk
1 tsp. vanilla extract
2 TBsps. Kirsch
2 squares unsweetened chocolate, melted
    and cooled slightly
1½ cups sifted cake flour
1½ tsps. baking powder
16½ oz. can dark sweet cherries, thoroughly
    drained

In a 9-inch round cake layer pan combine 4 tablespoons butter and ⅓ cup white sugar. Place in the oven to melt the butter. In the meantime, make the cake batter by creaming together the remaining butter and sugar. Add the egg, milk, vanilla, Kirsch and melted chocolate. Beat after each addition. Add the dry ingredients and combine thoroughly. Beat for one more minute. Stir the melted butter and sugar in the cake pan and place the cherries on top in an even layer. Spread the batter over the cherries. Use two spatulas if necessary (it is a rather stiff batter). Place the cake pan on a baking sheet to avoid splatters in the oven. Bake for about 30 minutes at 350 degrees, or until a toothpick inserted in the cake portion comes out clean. Cool. Cut into wedges and serve.

A cake known in Wolfpoint, Montana as "Erna's Cake." The recipe was given to me by Mary E. Smith. The filling and icing are mine. It is a sturdy pastry that lends itself well to frosting and decorating.

CITRUS BUTTERCREAM CHOCOLATE CAKE

Cake:

2 cups dark brown sugar
1 cup butter, softened
2 eggs
½ cup cocoa
1 cup buttermilk
2 tsps. soda
2 tsps. vanilla
2½ cups all-purpose flour
1 cup boiling water

Cream together the dark brown sugar and butter. Add the eggs one at a time, then add the other ingredients in order given. Beat very well after each addition. Finally, add the boiling water. Beat for one more minute and pour into two 9-inch round cake pans which have been buttered and sugared. Bake in a preheated oven at 350 degrees for 30-35 minutes, or until a toothpick inserted comes out clean. Cool in pans.

Frosting:

1 cup butter, softened
1⅔ cups confectioners' sugar
Finely grated zest of 2 oranges (orange part
    of the skin only)
Finely grated zest of 2 lemons (yellow part
    of the skin only)

Cream butter and sugar together and add the orange and lemon zest. Set aside until ready to use. For easy application do not refrigerate.

To assemble the cake:

Turn out the cake on a flat platter or tray covered with wax paper. Freeze the layers for one-half hour. Remove. Measure the thickness of the two layers and cut them to make the two perfectly even.

Trim the sides as well, if necessary. Gently brush off the crumbs and re-freeze the layers for one-half hour. In the meantime, create a cardboard base for the cake by tracing the outside of a cake pan on a sturdy piece of cardboard. Cut out and place on the serving plate; surround by strips of wax paper to keep frosting spills from dirtying the plate. This circle steadies the cake and prevents it from cracking. Remove cake layers from the freezer. Place one on the cardboard circle (save the prettiest for the top) and spread evenly with butter-cream frosting. Press the second layer on top and frost sides and top with remaining frosting.

Decoration:

Chocolate sprinkles
½ pint heavy cream
2 TBsps. white sugar

Apply the sprinkles by placing a handful at a time next to the cake and pressing them up into the frosted sides with a 6-7-inch long metal spatula. Whip the cream with the sugar. Spoon into a pastry bag with decorative tip. Outline the rim and embellish the top further with festive swirls and rosettes of cream. Remove wax paper strips and clean plate, if necessary. Refrigerate cake before serving.

The earthy flavor of pumpkin is combined with chocolate and pecans in the muffin recipe that follows. Together with a steaming cup of coffee, they will make a delightful surprise breakfast in bed for a special someone.

CHOCOLATE PECAN PUMPKIN MUFFINS

2½ cups sugar
1 cup salad oil
4 eggs
2 cups pumpkin, cooked and mashed or
    canned pumpkin
3 cups flour
½ tsp. baking powder
1 tsp. baking soda
½ tsp. salt
1½ tsps. cinnamon
1 tsp. nutmeg, freshly grated
1 cup pecans, chopped
1 cup mini chocolate chips

Combine sugar and oil; add eggs and beat until thoroughly incorporated; stir in

33

pumpkin. Sift together dry ingredients and add to sugar mixture. Add pecans and chocolate chips; stir to combine thoroughly. Fill muffin cups ¾ full. Bake at 350 degrees for 20-25 minutes, or until a toothpick inserted comes out clean. Serve warm or cold.

The following recipe for luscious mousse-brownies is coveted by all who frequent La Gourmandise, the delightful French bakery in White Plains, N.Y. I adapted it so that it can be made in a commonly available baking dish.

LA GOURMANDISE BROWNIES

1 cup lightly salted butter, softened
3 3-oz. bars bittersweet chocolate; use Callebeaut, Lindt or similar European chocolate, melted (see p. 10) and cooled
6 eggs, at room temperature
1¾ cups white sugar
¼ tsp. vanilla extract
2½ cups all-purpose flour
Confectioners' sugar
Pan: 3 qt. Pyrex baking dish—12″ x 8½″

Use a wire whisk to prepare this entire recipe. Combine butter and melted chocolate. In a separate bowl combine thoroughly the sugar and eggs, but do not overbeat. Stir in vanilla. Add flour, then chocolate mixture, to sugar and eggs. Again, do not overmix. Pour batter into buttered pan and bake in preheated oven at 300 degrees for 25-30 minutes. Do not overbake; these brownies should be soft in the middle. Cool. Dust heavily with confectioners' sugar. Refrigerate overnight. Cut into 1-inch squares.

The following delicately soft, not too sweet Chocolate Roll will be a favorite dessert in years to come.

CHOCOLATE ROLL

5 large eggs, separated
⅔ cup sugar
6 oz. semi-sweet chocolate
3 TBsps. strong coffee
Cocoa
1¼ cups heavy cream, whipped

Preheat the oven to 350 degrees.

Butter a large baking sheet measuring 8″ x 12″. Line it with wax paper and butter the paper. Beat the egg yolks and sugar with a rotary beater or electric mixer until thick and pale in color.

Combine the chocolate and coffee and place over low heat. Stir until chocolate melts (see p. 10). Let the mixture cool slightly, then stir it into the egg yolks. Beat the egg whites until stiff and fold them in. Spread the mixture evenly on the prepared baking sheet and bake 15 minutes, or until a knife inserted in the middle comes out clean. Do not over-bake.

Remove the pan from the oven and cover the cake with a damp cloth. Let stand 30 minutes or until cool. Loosen cake from the baking sheet and dust cake generously with cocoa. Turn the cake out on wax paper, cocoa side down, and carefully remove the paper from the bottom of the cake. Spread the cake with whipped cream, sweetened and flavored to taste, and roll up like a jelly roll. For easy rolling, firmly grasp each corner of the wax paper on which the cake was turned out and flip over about two inches of the edge on top of the cake. Continue to roll by further lifting the wax paper. The last roll should deposit the log on a long platter. Cover the top with whipped cream. Garnish with chocolate shavings. Serves 8.

The recipe that follows was devised in England during World War II. The fudge-like frosting is pure after-the-war exuberance.

WAR CHOCOLATE CAKE WITH POST-WAR FROSTING

Sift together in a large bowl:
1½ cups flour
2 heaping TBsps. cocoa
¼ tsp. salt
1 tsp. baking soda
1 cup sugar

Make a hole in the center and pour in:
½ cup vegetable oil
1 tsp. vanilla extract
1 cup warm water
1 TBsp. vinegar

Beat thoroughly with an electric beater. Bake in a buttered 8-inch square pan at 350 degrees for about 20 minutes. Remove, cool, and frost. Or, bake on a buttered 15"x10"x1" "jelly roll pan" for 15-20 minutes. When cool frost with a double batch of frosting. Cut into squares.

To Make the Frosting:

8 TBsps. butter, melted
¼ cup light brown sugar
2 cups confectioners' sugar

1½ TBsps. cocoa
2 TBsps. water
1 cup dry milk powder
1 tsp. vanilla extract

Combine all ingredients thoroughly to make a creamy frosting. Spread neatly onto cooled cake.

Barbara Kravitz

An Austrian confection that is neither a very large nor a very high cake, but the buttery crunch of the cookies and the smooth mocha cocoa cream of the filling yield so much pleasure that a small serving will suffice.

MOCHA COCOA COOKIE CAKE

2 cups flour
⅓ cup firmly packed brown sugar
11 TBsps. lightly salted butter
2 egg yolks, lightly beaten with a fork
1 tsp. vanilla extract
3 9-inch pie plates, buttered

Combine flour and sugar. With a dough-blender, or two knives, cut the butter into this mixture. Add the egg yolks and vanilla. Rub the dough between your fingers until it resembles coarse meal. Press it together into a ball. Divide into three parts. Press each part into the bottom of a pie plate. Do not make a rim.

You want a flat, large cookie. Bake for approx. 15 minutes at 325 degrees until lightly golden. Remove and cool.

To Make Mocha/Cocoa Buttercream:

½ cup butter, softened
1 cup confectioners' sugar
2 TBsps. cocoa
2 TBsps. coffee liqueur or 2 TBsps. very
strong coffee.

Combine all ingredients and beat with an electric beater until smooth.

To Make Coffee Glaze:

½ cup confectioners' sugar
1½-2 TBsps. coffee liqueur or 1½-2 TBsps
very strong coffee.

Add the coffee liqueur to the sugar a little at a time and stir to make a smooth glaze.

To Assemble the Cake:

Place a cookie on a plate; carefully spread it with half of the mocha/cocoa cream. Put another cookie on top; spread with the rest of the mocha/cocoa cream. Top with the third cookie. Spread coffee glaze on top layer. Cool in the refrigerator. Use a sharp, pointed knife for cutting. Serves 6.

Desserts

The recipe that follows won a silver cup a few years ago, and deservedly so. The exceptional blend of taste and textures raises the "common" pecan pie to new culinary heights.

ARIZONA PECAN CHOCOLATE RUM PIE

3 oz. unsweetened baking chocolate
6 TBsps. unsalted butter
5 eggs
1 cup dark brown sugar
1½ cups dark corn syrup
1½ tsps. vanilla extract
2 TBsps. rum (optional)
2½ cups pecans (approx. 10 oz.)
2 10-inch unbaked pie shells or 2 9-inch
    deep-dish unbaked pie shells

Melt chocolate and butter (see p. 10). Cool slightly. Beat eggs lightly and add to chocolate mixture. Then beat in sugar and corn syrup using a whisk. Mix in remaining ingredients and blend well. Pour into unbaked pie shells, dividing batter evenly. Bake at 400 degrees for 10 minutes, then at 350 degrees until set, about 30 minutes.

Jerome Soldevere

An adult dessert of sophisticated refinement. The barely discernible oatmeal gives body to the cream. The anise and orange combine in a digestive, fragrant blend of tastes. The smooth chocolate sauce enhances and rounds out the flavors.

CALEDONIA ICE WITH CHOCOLATE SAUCE

1 TBsp. sugar
1 cup heavy cream
5 TBsps. uncooked oatmeal, the quick cooking type
1 tsp. crushed anise seed
1 TBsp. grated orange zest (orange part of the skin only)

Add sugar to cream and whip until stiff. Fold in oatmeal, anise seed and orange zest. Freeze. Remove ½ hour before serving and refrigerate. Serve with chocolate sauce recipe which follows.

Elizabeth Remsen Van Brunt

The chocolate sauce works equally well with Caledonia Ice or with other recipes such as the Chocolate Souffle or the Majestic Pears. It is also a perfect topper for ice creams.

CHOCOLATE SAUCE

1 TBsp. butter
2 squares unsweetened chocolate
¾ cup sugar
¾ cup milk
¼ tsp. salt
½ tsp. vanilla

Melt the butter and chocolate (see p.
10). When melted, stir in the sugar and
milk alternately and a little at a time.
When all is combined stir in salt and vanilla. This makes a glossy, thick sauce.
Serve at room temperature. Serve in a
small pitcher with Caledonia Ice.

*Your guests will moan with delight when
you serve this outrageously delicious dish.
The light, fluffy peanut butter "cloud" surrounded by crisp crumbs and sweet chocolate is the ultimate indulgence.*

GIANT PEANUT BUTTER CUP

1½ cups creamy or crunchy peanut butter
½ cup confectioners' sugar
2 cups heavy cream, whipped to soft peaks
1 prepared chocolate crumb crust (use the
    recipe below, or a store-bought crust)
8 oz. sweet chocolate
4 TBsps. butter

43

Use an electric mixer to lighten the peanut butter. Beat in the sugar, then the whipped cream. Spread onto prepared chocolate crumb crust. Refrigerate. Combine the chocolate and butter. Melt and cool slightly (see p. 10); then spread evenly over the peanut butter filling. Cover the entire top. Refrigerate until the chocolate hardens, which will take about ½ hour. Cut with a pointed sharp knife into small servings.

Chocolate Crumb Crust:

1 cup chocolate cookie crumbs
1 TBsp. granulated sugar
3 TBsps. butter, melted and cooled

Combine the three ingredients and mix well. Press into the bottom and sides of a 9-inch pie plate. Bake at 350 degrees for about 10 minutes. Allow to cool; refrigerate.

Patricia C. Tabibian

The next recipe, created in the test kichens of the American Egg Board, is for a foolproof souffle. It is particularly good with the versatile Chocolate Sauce recipe (see p. 43).

HOT CHOCOLATE SOUFFLÉ

½ cup sugar, divided
⅓ cup unsweetened cocoa
¼ cup flour
⅛ teaspoon salt
1 cup milk
½ teaspoon vanilla
4 eggs, separated

In medium saucepan, combine 1/4 cup of the sugar, cocoa, flour and salt. Stir in milk. Cook over medium heat, stirring constantly, until mixture boils and is smooth and thickened. Stir in vanilla. Set aside. Prepare soufflé dish by buttering thoroughly and sprinkling with superfine sugar. In large mixing bowl, beat egg whites at high speed until foamy. Add remaining sugar, 2 tablespoons at a time, beating constantly until sugar is dissolved* and whites are glossy and stiff enough that they will not slip when the bowl is tilted. Thoroughly blend egg yolks into reserved sauce. Gently, but thoroughly, fold yolk mixture into whites. Carefully pour into 1½ to 2-quart soufflé dish or casserole. Bake in a preheated oven at 350 degrees until soufflé is puffy and delicately browned, and soufflé shakes slightly when oven rack is gently moved back and forth (about 30 to 40 minutes). Serve immediately.

*Rub just a bit of meringue between thumb and forefinger to feel if sugar has dissolved.

I would always hold my breath when my Mother would carefully bring the bowl of pudding to the table. Magically, it seemed, the two puddings did not mix. How delicious it was to create marble effects with the two creamy substances. A "nursery dessert" but a good one.

BLACK AND WHITE PUDDING

Vanilla Pudding:

1½ cups light cream, divided
2 TBsps. butter
1 TBsp. cornstarch
1½ TBsps. sugar
2 tsps. vanilla extract
2 eggs, lightly beaten with a fork

Bring 1¼ cups of cream with the butter to a boil. In the meantime, combine cornstarch and sugar; gradually add the remaining cream. Stir to make a smooth sauce. When the cream boils, reduce the heat and add the cornstarch mixture. Stir vigorously. Add the vanilla, and cook for one more minute. Reduce the heat to low. Add two tablespoons of pudding to the eggs and stir to combine; add this mixture to the rest of the pudding. Combine thoroughly. Gently cook for a few minutes, but do NOT boil. Remove and cool.

Chocolate Pudding:

1½ cups light cream, divided
2 TBsps. butter
1 TBsp. cornstarch
1½ TBsps. sugar
1½ TBsps. cocoa
2 eggs, lightly beaten with a fork

Bring 1¼ cups of cream with the butter to a boil. In the meantime, combine cornstarch, cocoa and sugar; gradually add the remaining cream. Stir to make a smooth sauce. When the cream boils, reduce the heat and add the cornstarch mixture. Stir vigorously. Reduce the heat to low. Add two tablespoons of pudding to the eggs and stir to combine; add this mixture to the rest of the pudding. Combine thoroughly; gently cook for a few minutes, while stirring, but do NOT boil. Remove and cool.

When both puddings are completely cooled, pour them at the same time from opposite sides into a bowl. They will meet in the middle. Do not mix. If desired, decorate with sweetened whipped cream (optional).

A marvellous children's dish, or a dessert to raise everyone's spirits.

Bright red, freshly poached pears, filled with a hazelnut-flavored truffle mixture, are placed in a smooth custard, which in turn is surrounded by a chocolate sauce. A perfect dessert for Christmas or any important day.

MAJESTIC PEARS

6 Bosc pears with stems
2 cups red wine
2 cups Grenadine syrup
1½ cups water
3 cups sugar
½ tsp. cinnamon
9 TBsps. Frangelico ganache, (See Melt-in-Your-Mouth Truffles recipe p. 18)
1 recipe Vanilla Custard (which follows)
Chocolate Sauce

Carefully peel the pears but leave them whole. Insert a small, sharp knife into bottom of pears and remove core. Create a neat hollow which will be filled later with ganache. Place the pears in a saucepan large enough to hold them in one layer. Add the red wine and Grenadine syrup. Poach the pears gently for about 20 minutes or until they are soft when pierced with a fork. In the meantime, bring the water, sugar and cinnamon to a boil. When the pears are soft, remove them to a large bowl. Pour in the sugar syrup and wine/Grenadine mixture. If necessary, place a plate on top of the pears to hold them down in the syrup. Refrigerate for 24 hours.

To serve: Remove pears from wine/Grenadine mixture and fill pears with the ganache. (Reserve marinating liquid for another use, if desired.) Divide Vanilla Custard among 6 serving dishes, spreading custard in a circle. Stand pear upright in center of custard. Surround custard with chocolate sauce. Serves 6.

Vanilla Custard:

1 cup whole milk
1 cup half and half
4 egg yolks
4 TBsps. sugar
1 tsp. vanilla extract

In the top of a double boiler, bring the milk and half and half to a boil. Beat together the egg yolks and sugar. Add some of the hot milk and combine. Stir the mixture into remaining hot milk. Simmer, stirring constantly, until the eggs coat the spoon and the sauce has thickened slightly. Add vanilla. Use as described above.

Marvin M. Maile

Add a new dimension to your backyard cooking and bring your deep fryer or electric frying pan outside. The two most bothersome aspects of deep frying are splatters that stain and smells that stay in the house. Both are eliminated when you move outdoors. The coated ice cream balls can be made ahead and frozen until ready to use.

DEEP FRIED CHOCOLATE ICE CREAM

4 TBsps. boiling water
10 TBsps. honey
2 cups finely crushed corn flakes
2 TBsps. cinnamon
1 quart chocolate ice cream
Vegetable oil

Combine the boiling water and honey and stir until mixture is very liquid. Add mixture to the finely crushed corn flakes and the cinnamon and stir to combine.

Now, recruit two other persons. You need one person to make ice cream balls with a proper ice cream scoop, the second to coat the balls with the corn flake and honey mixture; and the third to place the balls in the freezer as soon as they are made—otherwise they melt. With your helpers all lined up, follow this procedure:

Place a cookie sheet in the freezer. Place the coating mixture on a plate. Add an ice cream ball and roll to coat as evenly as possible. After each ball is coated place on the cookie sheet in the freezer. After a few hours, turn balls over so bottoms freeze. The balls must be frozen solid.

Heat oil in deep fryer to 350 degrees. Insert one ball in the oil at a time, count to 10, turn, and count to 10 again.

Remove with a slotted spoon and place on a plate covered with several layers of paper towels. Drain briefly and then serve on a small dish to a lucky guest. Makes 6 balls.

Serve the next orange-flavored chocolate custard in pretty cups. Top with a dollop of cream and sprinkle with a few candied orange strips. The recipe was created by the Gastronomy Director of Cointreau, the original orange liqueur from France.

MEXICAN CHOCOLATE POTS

1 navel orange
3 TBsps. light corn syrup
½ cup water
6 TBsps. Cointreau, divided
3 egg yolks
1 whole egg
⅓ cup sugar
2 cups milk
4 squares (1 oz. each) unsweetened
   chocolate

Remove rind from orange with vegetable peeler. Cut rind into thin strips. In a small saucepan combine corn syrup and water; bring to a boil. Add 3 TBsps. Cointreau and rind; simmer for 20 minutes or until rind is translucent. Drain. Preheat oven to 400 degrees.

In medium bowl, beat egg yolks, whole egg and sugar until well blended. In a small saucepan, heat milk and chocolate over moderate heat (see p. 10). Stir until chocolate has melted and is well blended. Slowly pour into beaten egg mixture, beating constantly. Add orange rind (but keep enough for garnish) and remaining liqueur; blend well.

Pour into 6 well-buttered custard cups. Place in hot water bath. Bake for 40 minutes, or until set. Do not overbake. Makes 6 servings.

A mouth-watering French classic.

CHOCOLATE MOUSSE

4 oz. semi-sweet chocolate morsels
5 eggs, separated
3 TBsps. sugar
½ pint heavy cream
2 TBsps. brandy

Melt chocolate chips in top of double boiler. Remove chocolate from stove and add beaten egg yolks. Mix thoroughly. In another bowl add sugar to heavy cream and beat until whipped. Add whipped cream to chocolate mixture. Beat egg whites until stiff. Fold egg whites into chocolate mixture. Add brandy. Pour into serving bowl, and refrigerate for at least 10 hours.

An appropriate variation on an old theme.
Both the slightly tart raspberries and the
"bite" of the liqueur prevent this dish from
becoming cloyingly sweet.

CHOCOLATE TRIFLE WITH RASPBERRIES

1 half-inch thick slice stale chocolate cake
1½ cups stale chocolate cake, cut into small
   cubes
2 oz. Creme de Cocoa
½ cup sliced toasted almonds
1 10-oz. package frozen unsweetened
   raspberries, thawed
1-2 TBsps. sugar
Chocolate Pudding (see recipe below)
½ pint heavy cream
2 TBsps. sugar

Place the slice of chocolate cake in the
bottom of a glass dish. It should be big
enough to cover the bottom completely.
Scatter the cake cubes on top and pour
the liqueur over the cake. Leave it to
soak for one-half hour. Sprinkle with the
toasted almonds. Gently combine the
thawed berries with 1-2 tablespoons sugar. Reserve some of the prettiest berries
and some of the juice for the top and
spoon the remainder over the almonds.

Top with chocolate pudding which is made as follows:

Chocolate Pudding:

1½ cups whole milk, divided
1 TBsp. butter
1½ TBsps. cocoa
1 TBsp. cornstarch
1½ TBsps. sugar
1 tsp. vanilla

Bring 1¼ cups of milk with the butter to a boil. In the meantime, combine cocoa, cornstarch and sugar; gradually add the remaining milk. Stir to make a smooth sauce. When the milk boils, reduce heat and add the chocolate mixture. Stir vigorously. Add vanilla. Cook for one more minute. Remove from heat and pour over the raspberries. Cool. While the pudding is cooling whip the cream with the sugar. When cool, top the pudding with the cream. Decorate with the reserved berries and drizzle with the juice.

Drinks

An old story with a new twist.

MOSCOW MOCHA

1½ oz. vodka
¾ oz. chocolate liqueur
¾ oz. coffee liqueur

Shake together and pour over ice into a short rocks glass and mix.

Named for Dr. Norman J. Larson, known for his home-made Curacao, this smooth cold drink with its lingering orange flavor is perfect for a moonlit summer night on the terrace. It can serve as both an after-dinner drink or dessert.

NORMAN'S DREAM

1½ oz. Curacao
1 generous scoop of chocolate ice cream

Place in the blender and blend until just smooth. Pour into a champagne glass. Top with whipped cream, chocolate shavings and grated orange zest, if desired. It is quite good without these trimmings.

You'll dream of palm trees, a full moon and tropical beaches when you sip the next drink. A small dish of banana chips is the perfect accompaniment.

TRADEWIND

1 oz. rum
1 oz. Creme de Banana
1 oz. chocolate liqueur

Blend in a blender together with 3 ice cubes. Pour into short rocks glass.

A slushy, creamy, almond-flavored treat that goes down so very easily.

NUTTY COCO-CREAM

1½ oz. almond liqueur
1½ oz. chocolate liqueur
3 oz. heavy cream

Blend in blender together with 4 ice cubes. Pour into 8 oz. glass.

For lovers of anise, the perfect after-dinner drink is made as follows:

ROMAN CANDLE

1½ oz. Sambucca

1½ oz. chocolate liqueur
½ oz. Irish Cream

Pour the Sambucca and chocolate liqueur into a cordial glass. Pour in the Irish Cream over the back of a spoon.

A luscious, lethal "milk shake" that should be sipped slowly.

WHITE MOCHA DELIGHT

1 oz. vodka
2 oz. chocolate liqueur
1½ oz. coffee liqueur
2 oz. milk

Blend in a blender with 3 ice cubes. Pour into 8 oz. glass.

The haunting delicacy of the dusting of cinnamon rounds out the assembled flavors.

CINNAMON MOCHA

6 oz. hot chocolate drink
1½ oz. coffee liqueur
Whipped cream
Cinnamon

Combine chocolate and liqueur in a coffee mug. Top with cream. Dust with cinnamon. Sprinkle on some shaved chocolate if desired. Serve with a cinnamon stick for stirring.

A warming drink for a devilishly cold night.

DOUBLE DEVIL

¾ oz. almond liqueur
¾ oz. chocolate liqueur
¾ oz. coffee liqueur
6 oz. hot coffee
Whipped cream, if desired

Combine the liqueurs; add the coffee. Serve in a mug with cream, if desired.

The rum cuts the sweetness of the syrup in this hot coffee drink.

MEXICAN COFFEE

5 oz. hot coffee
1 oz. chocolate syrup (or Chocolate Sauce, see p. 43)
1½ oz. rum

Combine the ingredients and top with whipped cream. Serve in a coffee mug.

A nutty hot toddy for those who want to avoid coffee.

TOASTED ALMOND

1 oz. chocolate liqueur
1 oz. almond liqueur
Hot water
A little milk
Whipped cream, if desired

Combine the liqueurs, add hot water and milk to make an 8-oz. drink. Top with cream. Serve in a coffee mug.

For that horrible moment when there is not a speck of chocolate in the house, Hannah Glasse in her book The Art of Cookery Made Plain and Easy, published in 1796, devised a drink to stave off that feeling of panic.

SHAM CHOCOLATE

Take a pint of milk, boil it over a slow fire with some whole cinnamon, and sweeten it with Lisbon sugar; beat up the yolks of three eggs, throw all together into a chocolate pot and mill it one way, or it will turn. Serve it up in chocolate cups.

Menus for Chocolate Occasions

BREAKFAST IN BED:
Just a little chocolate to start the day
Sham Chocolate (p. 61)
Sliced Kiwi
Chocolate Pecan Pumpkin
    Muffins (p.33)
Butter Curls

BRUNCH:
A chocolate twist to this popular Sunday
    entertainment
Cinnamon Mocha (p.59)
Mexican Chocolate Pots (p.52)
Mosaic Cookies (p.26)
Chocolate Almond Crunchies (p.22)
Chocolate Fruit Delight (p.15)
Hot Rolls with Orange Marmalade and
    Chocolate/Hazelnut Spread
Butter Curls

CHILDREN'S PARTY:

For the young ones who love chocolate
Chocolate-Coated Strawberries (p.17)
Deep Fried Chocolate Ice Cream (p.50)
Monster Cookies (p.25)
Chocolate Milk

WINTER DESSERT PARTY:

A good fundraiser for your favorite charity
Double Devil (p.60)
Coffee or Tea
Arizona Pecan Chocolate Rum Pie (p.41)
Giant Peanut Butter Cup (p.43)
Citrus Buttercream Chocolate
    Cake (p.30)
Classic Truffles (p.13)

SUMMER DESSERT PARTY:

To be served by moonlight on the terrace
White Mocha Delight (p.59)
Iced Tea or Coffee
Nutty Coco-Cream (p.58)
Caledonia Ice with Chocolate
    Sauce (p.42)

Mocha Cocoa Cookie Cake (p.38)
Deep Fried Chocolate Ice Cream (p.50)
Chinese Torture (p.16)
Chocolate Swirl Lace Cookies (p.23)

CHOC-TAIL PARTY:

What else would you call a cocktail party with chocolate drinks?

Norman's Dream (p.57)
Moscow Mocha (p.57)
Roman Candle (p.58)
Tradewind (p.58)
Candied Pineapple
Banana Chips
Assorted Nuts
Melt-In-Your-Mouth Truffles (p.18)
Double Chip Cookies (p.24)